Fortnite

Battle Royale

A Complete How-to-Win Guide
Updated for Season 6

By: Premiere Game GuideX

FORTNITE BATTLE ROYALE

A COMPLETE HOW-TO-WIN GUIDE
UPDATED FOR SEASON 6

PREMIERE GAME GUIDEX

TABLE OF CONTENTS

Contents

Introduction..7

So What's New in Season 6? 10

New Places in Season 6:....................10

The Corrupted Zones........................10

The Floating Lake House...................12

The Castle at Haunted Hills.............13

Tomato Temple 13

Loot Lake Becomes Leaky Lake......14

The New Weapons and Items in Season 6:.......15

The Shadow Stones 15

The Port-a-Fortress 17

The Heavy Sniper............................17

The Shockwave Grenade 18

The Grappler 18

The Quad Launcher 19

The Rift-to-Go 19

The Chiller 20

How to Win in Fortnite: Battle Royale **22**

How to Win Solo Games **22**

Strategy 1: The Slow Bird (Easiest Strategy) 24

Strategy 2: The Rim Rider (Beginner Level) 25

Strategy 3: The Sneak (Intermediate)..............26

Strategy 4: Follow the Bull (Advanced) 27

Strategy 5: The Ninja (Expert) 28

How to Win Any Game mode **31**

Practice 31

Guarantee Yourself a Weapon 31

Build..32

Think Logically...33

Use the Shadow Stones...................................34

Advanced Techniques **35**

    Building 35

    Combat.. 36

    Surviving... 38

    Looting 41

Tips and Tricks for Every Player & Mode **44**

Thank You For Purchasing!

Premiere Game GuideX would like to personally thank you for downloading an ebook or purchasing a paperback copy of our game guide. We aim to satisfy our readers and enhance the abilities of fellow gamers alike.

Gamers have more fun when they actually know how to play the game which is where we come in. Our game guides will unlock the secrets to achieving mastery level and give you the perfect strategies to win! Please be on the look out for even more game guides in the future!

Thanks again!,

Premiere Game GuideX

Introduction

Fortnite, publicly released in 2017 by Epic Games, is now the most popular battle royale game in the world and it is still free to play. If you haven't played Fortnite yet, you can find it for free on Windows, Mac, PlayStation 4, Xbox One, Nintendo Switch and even iOS and Android devices! You have most likely seen the cultural impact this game has had if you're on social media and it's not for just any reason; Fortnite has won numerous awards including *2017's Best Multiplayer* by *The Game Awards.* In the last year alone, Fortnite has drawn in more than 125 million people–all attempting to achieve the oh-so-coveted *Victory Royale.*

An amazing uniqueness about Fortnite is the constant updates and changes brought on by Epic Games on a regular basis. The Battle Royale game mode is following a story as time goes on and changes seasons around every 6 weeks. There are also many small changes or "soft updates" Epic Games will put in during seasons but you can expect much bigger changes from season to season. At the end of Season 4 and beginning of 5, there were rifts created in the sky by a rocket launched from the Evil Lair. These rifts, which are not much rarer, can be used to teleport you into the sky, allowing you to fly away from danger. Then, Season 5 was amazing as expected; it included the addition of Viking characters and a Viking village stranded on the top of a mountain and other Warrior characters to play at. There was also the biggest change; the addition of the area that consumes 1/5 of the map now, Paradise Palms and the amazing golf carts. At the end of Season 5, we saw a large bolt of energy come out of the main rift in the center of the sky created in Season 4 and pull a mysterious purple cube from the ground. The context for Season 6 was revealed.

In this book we will be showing you how to win in Fortnite's Battle Royale Mode as a Solo, Duo, and Squad and all especially updated for the Season 6 changes.

So What's New in Season 6?

There are a bunch of changes in Season 6–so many that the gameplay, special skills, and tactics you can use have actually changed significantly. There are over 10 new weapon items in this season, the removal of a few favorites, and several new places to fight your battles and loot your supplies. Some of these new weapons can change your game experience and result dramatically as long as you beat the learning curve and get better with them faster than the other millions of players.

New Places in Season 6:

The Corrupted Zones

Already included in Week 2 of this season's challenges, there are 7 new corrupted zones for you to visit. These zones are uniquely new to Season 6 and are littered with the mysterious purple cubes and force you to find all over the map. While these zones are definitely hot spots and not recommended for cautious gameplay, the loot there is pretty awesome. Typically, they will have 2-5 chests in each zone. They are also littered with geysers filled with a purple glowing lava-like liquid that shoots you up into the air when you jump on it. Finally, the main attractions of the corrupted zones, the Shadow Stones that give you super powers.

You can find the corrupted zones:

- Between *Greasy Grove and Shifty Shafts*
- *Between Fatal Fields and Salty Springs*
- *Another one between Salty Springs and Dusty Divot*
- *Between the desert landscape and Retail Row*
- *In Wailing Woods*

- *Between Lazy Links, The Tomato Temple, and Leaky Lake*
- *Finally, Southwest of Pleasant Park, next to the mountain with the evil lair.*

The Floating Lake House

Surrounded and lifted by a purple tornado, the house that was once a beautiful property on Loot Lake, is now a magnificent property floating in the sky. At the beginning of the season, this house was floating above what is now Leaky Lake. As of now at the time of writing, this tornado has travelled over to Wailing Woods and is floating there for now.

Loot Lake becomes Leaky Lake. You can land on the house directly from the Battle Bus or simply walk into the tornado from the ground and fly up yourself. There is no real risk when using the tornado because you can deploy your parachute at any time just like when using a launch pad. This tornado is an amazing way to outrun the incoming storm if you procrastinated your getaway.

The Castle at Haunted Hills

There is also a brand-new castle on top of the mountain right next to Haunted Hills. This new map location is pretty big but nothing special stands out about it. At the moment, because it is a brand new location, you can expect it to be significantly more crowded. But in the future, because it is located on the outskirts of the map, it may make a nice unnamed location for easy looting in the future. There has also been a lot of speculation as to whether it will be upgraded and turned into a completely new location name called "Crazy Castle."

Tomato Temple

The beloved Tomato Town is no more. Now, it has been replaced by a temple dedicated to the praise of tomatoes and Tomato Head. Here you can find ancient ruins with tons of loots all around a giant pyramid loaded with secret passages, rooms and loot spots. When you are in the temple, be sure to look in every direction for any secret rooms or passages because there are tons!

Loot Lake Becomes Leaky Lake

The place once known as Loot Lake has now suffered trauma in Season 6 as the purple vortex sucks all the water down like a drain. When the property and land in the middle of the lake floated away, the destructive process started. However, you can use the middle to your advantage because if you jump in the center of the vortex, you will be shot up into the sky and be allowed to parachute away. There is also typically a lot of chests surrounding the middle but be careful because this is definitely a hot spot.

The New Weapons and Items in Season 6:

The Shadow Stones

Found in the corrupted zones, are the newly added Shadow Stones. The Shadow Stones are consumables just like apple and mushrooms; but they give you superpowers instead of more health and shield. When you consume a Shadow Stone, you transform into a ghost-like creature that is nearly invisible to everyone else. This mode of character gives you faster speeds, invisibility, and the ability to phase through objects. You can also exit the mode of character at any time, which makes it especially useful in combat. A great way to get surprise attack kills is to phase through a wall as a ghost, exit the ghost mode quickly, and then immediately fire at your opponent. You will have to do this fast, however, because as a ghost, your only nearly invisible and your only defense is a quick getaway which is sometimes not enough.

The Port-a-Fortress

The addition of the Port-a-Fort changed the game by allowing less skill players to not be so easily overtaken by another players more advanced building skills. The Port-a-Fortress multiplies the advantage of the Port-a-Fort exponentially! The Port-a-Fortress instantly creates a huge fort 5 times the size of a regular Port-a-Fort. This item is a gold item so it's a little rarer to find.

The Heavy Sniper

This weapon delivers an insane amount of damage, 150-157 for opponents and 1,050-1,100 for structures. That means it can destroy every type of wall on any building in the game in one shot–the only exception are the metal storage containers. While the damage from this weapon is amazing, the reload time is very slow so you better be sure you are going to hit your target in one or maybe two shots.

The Shockwave Grenade

This weapon is capable of launching people and vehicles far away without having any fall damage. The traditional impulse grenades will cause you or an opponent to have fall damage. You can find these in stacks of two and have a maximum of 6 at a time.

The Grappler

The Grappler is a new way for you to gain the upper hand if your building skills are lacking. As we will talk about later, a height advantage is a crucial aspect in winning any Fortnite battle and the Grappler can allow you to get to new heights with a single press. The Grappler works with a plunger and comes with 10 uses. You can't find any ammo for this item; but at the same time, if you fire the plunger and it doesn't end up sticking to a surface, you won't have lost any uses.

The Quad Launcher

The Quad Launcher is a sweet weapon that allows you to rapidly fire RPGs at your opponent 4 at a time. While you may think this weapon will give you a great advantage, it however has a very low damage and would be better used to quickly destroy enemy structures and make them fall, then to directly hit them. A direct hit with one of these rockets for example will only result around 80 damages.

The Rift-to-Go

With the reduced amount of rifts found throughout the landscape, there has come the item that does it for you. When you use one, you create a rift that lasts 10 seconds, allowing other players to use it as well. What's awesome about this rift is you can use it no matter where you are and as an instant getaway if you are facing otherwise certain death.

The Chiller

A whole new trap has been added to the game this season; the Chiller. The Chiller is an ice trap—as you probably guessed—and it puts ice blocks on the feet of anyone, including you, who steps foot on it. The ice blocks can be a disadvantage and an advantage. You can use these slippery tools to make enemies fall from high structures to their death or even let yourself slide super speed down a large ramp. To do the super speed slide, make a long downward track and place an ice trap at the top. When you slide down, you will even keep sliding on the grass and can make it a significant distance!

Like always, we have to say goodbye to some weapons and items as well. On the removed list in Season 6: traditional impulse grenades, the suppressed submachine gun, the light machine gun—also known as the Tommy

Gun—and the Remote Explosives, also known as C4s. The removal of these items may not be permanent and just for Season 6, epic frequently does this to change up the game play, make room for new weapons and items, but sometimes to also remove over-powered or faulty weaponry as well.

How to Win in Fortnite: Battle Royale

Only one to four people can win a regular game of Fortnite at a time which is part of what makes a Victory Royale so special. If you implement the right strategies and take the right approach, you can significantly increase your chances of winning again and again. It's a big claim, but here we will tell you how to win in the three main modes Fortnite Battle Royale offers: Solo, Duos, and Squads.

How to Win Solo Games

Winning a solo game is the best feeling ever because you know that you yourself beat 99 other individuals at something—now that's something to be proud of! Because Solo wins are the most important, here we will list the top 5 different strategies you can use or modify to increase your chances of winning. The strategies will be listed in the order of easiest/least experience needed to difficult/advanced abilities required and are typically effective in getting you to the last 5 players. At that point, you are usually forced to utilize building skills or just fight back.

Quickly before we list the top 5 strategies for a solo win, there are constants that should be applied to any game where the player is serious about winning.

Follow these steps in every strategy at the beginning of every game:

1. Scan for nearby opponents as you land.
2. Find a Shotgun, Compact SMG, Suppressed Pistol, or Dual Pistols.
3. Collect 200 Wood.
4. Find an Assault Rifle.
5. Find a Shield.
6. Collect 200 Wood.

Strategy 1: The Slow Bird (Easiest Strategy)

When your goal is to simply get a win–with no need for a bunch of kills–the Slow Bird Strategy can be perfect for you, especially if you are inexperienced as well. The Slow Bird Strategy involves you waiting until the very end of the Battle Bus ride and deploying your chute instantly as you exit the bus. From here, try not to move at all and let yourself gently float down. If you watch the player count, wait until there are 65-75 players left and then look for a landing spot. Try finding a corrupted zone to land at so you can become a ghost or find a remote spot with no given name. Gently glide over there with as little movement and speed as possible. By the time you land, there will only be less than 60 players left already. If you are going to use this strategy, you should probably follow strategy number 2 or 3 for the next portion of the match.

Strategy 2: The Rim Rider (Beginner Level)

You can implement this strategy before or after you jump off the Battle Bus. If you do it before, pick a spot on the outskirts of the map to increase your chances of being outside of the circle that game. As the storm comes in, constantly remain right in front of the boundary. When the storm is stationary, you should remain within half grid block of the boundary the whole time but also keep moving clockwise or counterclockwise around the circle boundary making sure not to stay still too long.

If you are lucky enough to find a Chug Jug or Med Kit and a Golf Cart early on in the game while using this strategy, you can allow yourself to be consumed by the storm and ride out just before. This is risky of course because if anyone sees you, it won't take much to kill you. But people tend to stay away from the storm so it's more likely you won't see anyone. Of course, use the Med Kit as soon as you are out of the storm.

Strategy 3: The Sneak (Intermediate)

Similar to the Rim Rider, this strategy focuses on minimal engagement and avoiding unnecessary conflict. Try staying in the wooded areas looting and collecting Wood for the first half of the match, then move your way into buildings. Utilize the spaces under stairways and behind furniture to surprise any opponents who enter the house. While you are in the wooded areas, it's best to have a medium ranged weapon equipped like an Assault Rifle; but in closer quarters and indoors a Shotgun or Combat SMG will be better. Suppressed Pistols and Dual Pistols also deliver good amounts of damage and they have a high fire rate and are relatively easy to aim—the faster your trigger finger, the more effective these two weapons are. You can land anywhere using this strategy but again, remote places tend to be safer.

Strategy 4: Follow the Bull (Advanced)

If you have more advanced capabilities and are able to not only effectively attack and defend in one-on-one combat but also outbuild the average player, then you should give this strategy a try. Start by picking a player in the sky as you jump off of the Battle Bus and following them at a safe distance. Still perform the start of game duties like finding a Shotgun and getting 200 Wood, but always know where the player you spotted is. Follow this player as they collect materials and loot for you the whole time. If the player you are following gets attacked by others, perform a tactical retreat and gain high ground to watch the events unfold. Whoever the battle winner is, it's your new bull to follow. Rinse and repeat this process until there are roughly 20 players left. At this point start looking for the best sneak attack opportunity you can on this player knowing they will have copious amounts of loot for you if you are successful. After the 20 players left the checkpoint, it's best to implement a safer strategy like #3 or #2.

Strategy 5: The Ninja (Expert)

Coined after the famous Ninja himself, this strategy is only for the most experienced players. When implementing this strategy, you will want to stock up on things like the Shockwave Grenades, Bounce Pads, Launch Pads, Rift-to-Go's, Ice Traps and Material. Still avoiding unnecessary drama, you can focus on refining your ability to use launching equipment to your advantage. Always keep the Shockwave Grenades handy in order to penetrate enemy forts or to allow yourself a quick getaway. This strategy entails your implementing traits from strategy #4 for the first portion of the game, and then your primary focus will be on building complex structures.

As you near the end of the game, build large structures that will be almost impossible to knockdown. You can do this by creating numerous anchors to the ground and surroundings in multiple places while also doubling up on walls and building "fake" structures next to the one you inhabit, so it's harder for opponents to find out where you are.

How to Win Duo and Squad Games

When playing with partners or groups, you can actually all follow the above strategies together as a team. What these game modes will require, however, is adequate communication and the assigning of roles and responsibilities. As the game starts and your group or pair has picked their strategy, assign roles to each player. Try and assign roles that are best suited for individual players. For example, if you know your friend *Minnoxide* is better at sniping, let them carry all heavy bullets and snipers. If your friend *Fudgenuttz* can build like a god, then assign them to collecting extra material at the beginning of the game while you or someone else goes and finds good weapons and lot for them. You can also divvy up the way your group carries resources. Instead of everyone having some band aids, for example, have one person for medical stuff and one person for shields.

During combat in these modes, it's important to use the numbers you have as an advantage. Communicate where each of you are during a battle and attempt to surround enemies leaving them no room for retreat. Groups also have the huge advantage of distraction; you can have one player fire an ammo heavy weapon like a Minigun while the other player travels around to the opposite side of the opponent for a surprise attack from behind.

How to Win Any Game mode

Practice

If you are serious about winning, which I am sure you are because you have this book, then practice is what you will need to do. You can use the Playground mode for this and practice aiming while jumping and running without worrying about dying and having to restart in a new lobby. If you have friends, playground practice can be much more effective as long as you limit the area to a certain size. You can also try raising your standards of difficulty. By this, I mean try playing some solo games on the Squads mode. This will probably force you to be in situations where it is 2-4 vs. 1, and if you can get yourself used to this, one-on-one battles will be a walk in the park.

Guarantee Yourself a Weapon

When landing, scout everywhere in the zone you have chosen and keep in mind the previous games you have played. Ask yourself; "Where were the chests before? Is there usually a Shotgun in this room? Haven't I found a big Shield here before?" While the item and weapon spawning is random, there is still some tendency for the same weapon to show up in the same spot in multiple games.

If you're landing where buildings are, **always try to land on the roof.** The attic in many houses can contain a chest but also provides safe passage into the top floor of the house. Once you have a weapon on top, you now have the immediate height advantage over anybody who landed nearby.

Build

Hone in on your building skill—it's the most important part about Fortnite. In any battle, the winner or winners are typically determined by who could get the greater height advantage. It's always going to be easier to shoot someone below then to shoot someone above. If you haven't already, switch your control layout to "Builder Pro", which will allow you to switch between and place structures at a much faster rate.

An essential structure you need to teach yourself to build is the ramp + wall combo. Place a vertical wall and then quickly place a ramp on it and keep doing this upwards to gain the height advantage on your opponent. The wall in front of each ramp as you go up will make it much more difficult for you to get shot down. When you can, attach your ramp to their structure from above so as to make sure you don't fall down.

Think Logically

As mentioned before, avoid the unnecessary drama. If you see opponents who are out of your way and of no immediate threat, just leave them alone while also making sure you know where they are. Try and also make good judgement calls when you are landing in a more crowded place. If you see someone racing down with their chute for the same weapon you are, just divert your direction and avoid the chance of them getting their first.

Use the Shadow Stones

It's not just faster speeds and invisibility you get with the "Ghost Mode". You are also able to reach new heights! If you consume a Shadow Stone and then jump into a geyser, you will reach heights higher than many of the mountain peaks on the map. While in the air you can trigger your phase and semi-fly through the air but most definitely levitate and scan the surrounding area! There is also no need to worry about running out of time because you still don't take any fall damage when the ghost wears off.

Advanced Techniques

Building

When you get a bit more advanced, you can practice moves commonly known as the "double push" and "triple push." The double push is when you have to ramps side by side, with the wall barrier in front, three levels up. A triple push would be the more advanced move with a ramp + wall + floor combo. This move prevents the enemy from running underneath the ramp and bypassing the wall barrier, or at least adds another layer of resistance. Practice these structures in Playground mode and then take it to the battle field; but fair warning, you got to be fast!

When you make it to the final circle and it happens to be in an open area, bombard the field with walls and structures. This will pre-set the tone and direction of the game later in your favor when the enemies' structures are built on top and throughout your already existing structures. This is because you can now edit the walls and find enemies who are hiding between walls, or even knock down the entire structure and kill them off that way.

Combat

One great combo to practice would be the Shockwave Grenade + Shotgun combo. This involves you placing down a Shockwave Grenade in the perfect position to launch you towards your enemy at full speed. Not only will this most likely fluster your opponent and cause them to panic, but you also gain the height advantage as you come flying in. This will take a lot of in-game practice to get right, especially the aiming of one shot you get with your Shotgun. If you are confident with your aiming abilities, I recommend using a Pump Shotgun because they have a longer range, but if aiming is something you struggle with I recommend a Tactical or Heavy Shotgun.

You also want to master the double pump. For this you will need to pump Shotguns and need to place them side by side in your inventory. When you shoot your enemy with one shot of the pump, quickly switch to your other pump bypassing the reload time and striking the enemy once again. When the double pump is mastered it can bring a devastating amount of damage. There is also something called the "Quick Switch." The Quick Switch is when you strike an enemy at close range with a weapon designed to take maximum damage, like a Sniper Rifle, and then immediately switching to an Assault Rifle or close-range weapon to finish the opponent off.

Not a lot of people utilize this technique which is sure to give you the upper hand. You know how when you edit a wall it becomes clear for a second? Well, you can use that trait to your advantage and when trapped in your own structure by spying on the opponent's position. Simply open the builder without changing anything on the actual wall.

At the same time, while you are pushing an enemy base, always go for the ground floor or middle ground to knock their structure over. Placing one vertical wall behind you, and then running forward while attaching roofs to that wall can be an effective way for you to get close to the enemies base ground floor. Be careful as to not attach this to the enemies' base, because it will just act as an anchor.

Surviving

During combat and gameplay, you should always be aware of your location on the map in relation to the safe zone and the storm. Start doing some mental math and calculate how long it will take you to run from where you are to the safe zone. A grid square on the map is approximately 45 seconds of running on flat uninterrupted terrain. Of course, you will have to take into account the hills, lakes, canyons, and other obstacles, as well as the aids–like launch pads–you may have.

Make sure to always cover your tracks, especially when you are defenseless. At the beginning of the match, for example, make sure you close all doors behind you when you enter a house and break the stairs behind you when you go upstairs. Yes, your opponent can just build up to the second floor but the sound of them building will act as just another alarm telling you they are there.

While playing Duos or Squads, if you or one of your teammates has below 30 health, suicide should be committed. Because after you revive one another, you will have gained your health back up to at least 30. You can also use this technique to get out of the storm for a considerable distance. In fact, in the first and second storm (lower damage), two people can make it across the entire map dying and reviving, dying and reviving, over and over again. The key is to always have the individual with lower health run in front and to revive the second they are down.

Try storm diving. This is when you stock up on aids and get a Golf Cart then spend most of your time in the first two circles in the storms. The advantage here, of course, is that you will be free from enemy dangers; but if you run out of aids, then you're most likely a goner. Remember 45 seconds = one flat grid square.

Looting

Throughout the game, always make sure that you have adequate amounts of material at all times. If you prefer to land in areas with lots of building, get in the habit of breaking furniture as you loot a house. Furniture is much more efficient in stacking up Wood than you may think and if you do this in multiple houses early on—you should have 200 Wood super fast. On the other hand, if you have time to gather Brick or Metal, allow yourself the extra effort to stack up on those. Metal and Brick take a bit longer to get but significantly increase your defenses while you're in battle.

A good player will also never pass up readily available Ammo Boxes. Fortnite allows you to carry up to and over 1,000 Ammo supplies on many guns so take advantage of that and stock up. The extra ammo will come in handy when you need to destroy structures later on and still have enough to go in for the kill.

The successfulness of any Fortnite player will be determined on their uses of the above strategies and their ability to be honest with themselves. If you know you suck at using the Pump Shotgun but everyone says it is amazing, don't just buy into the hype. Utilize your strengths and mitigate your weaknesses while using all of the above tips, techniques, and strategies and, for sure....

You will win a Victory Royale!

Refer to the next page for a quick reference while you are in battle along with some awesome Fortnite pictures!

Tips and Tricks for Every Player & Mode

START EVERY GAME WITH THIS CHECKLIST:

1. Pick a strategy.
2. Decide where to land.
3. Find a Shotgun, Combat SMG, Suppressed Pistol, Dual Pistols, or any close-range weapons.
4. Collect 200 Wood.
5. Find Shields if you haven't yet.
6. Find a medium-range weapon.

ORGANIZE YOUR INVENTORY INTELLIGENTLY

While it may be tempting to have 5 powerful weapons at once, it's not practical for obtaining a Victory Royale. Make sure you have at least

ALWAYS LAND ON THE ROOF

House attics usually contain chests and landing on a roof will give you the height advantage right from the beginning.

BUILD, BUILD, BUILD!

USE YOUR SURROUNDINGS

When inside houses, use windows to scope out your enemies or edit windows in your structures to defend your base. Make sure you also scope through windows to see if anyone is being careless and peeking out.

IF YOU CAN'T HAVE IT. NO ONE CAN!